WHY WE LOVE BASKETBALL

BLACK RABBIT BOOKS

AIDAN WHITCOMB

TABLE OF CONTENTS

1. James and the Peach Basket 4

2. Inside the Arena 6

3. Sensational Superstars 8

4. Dramatic Dunks 12

5. Welcome to the W 15

6. March Madness 19

More to Explore 22

1

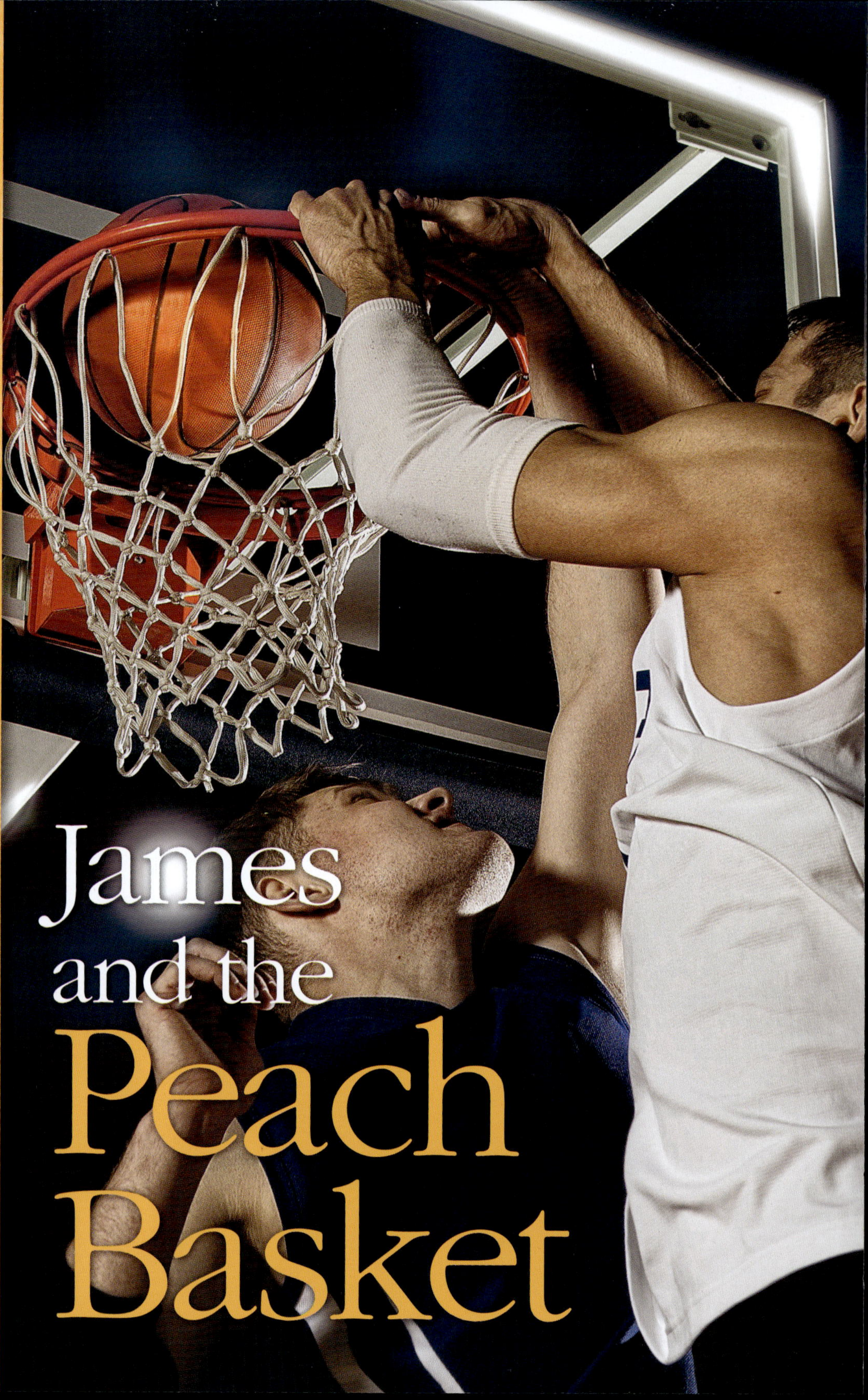

James and the Peach Basket

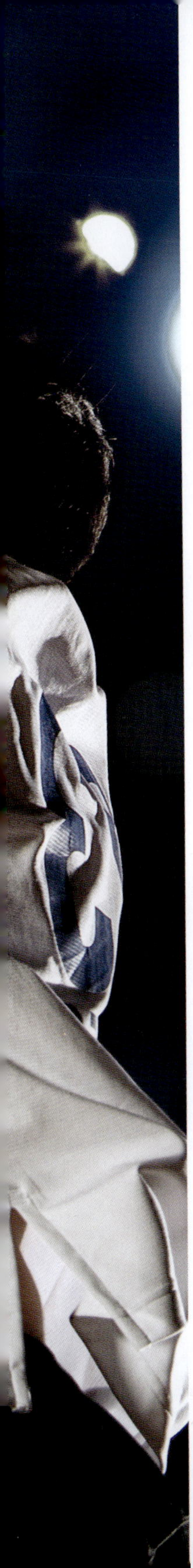

Basketball has a rich history. It was invented by James Naismith in 1891. Naismith used peach baskets for hoops. Now hoops look different. They have steel rims and glass backboards.

Much has changed since 1891. In 1949, the National Basketball Association (NBA) was created. The new **league** drew in fans. The sport grew quickly. In 2024, 22.5 million fans attended games. Basketball has fans of all ages.

Statue of James Naismith and a peach basket

2

Inside the Arena

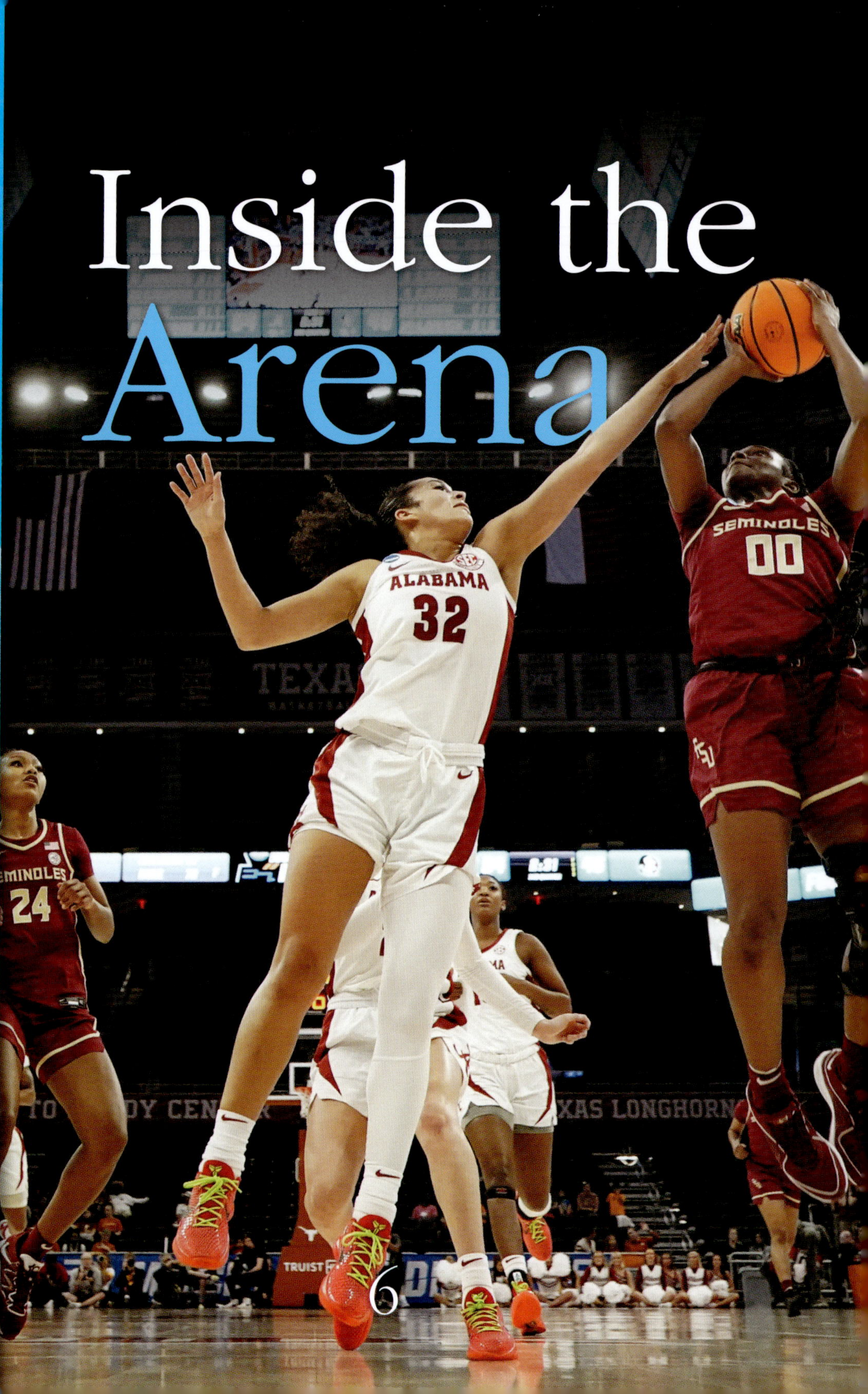

Basketball is a great sport to watch live. Basketball games are fast-paced. There are powerful dunks. Players shoot long three-pointers. Basketball arenas are lively. Fans cheer loudly. They try to get on the jumbotron.

Basketball players love their fans. Some players take pictures with fans. Some sign balls, jerseys, and hats. Many celebrities are fans. Everyone loves watching the sport's best!

Did You Know?

There are 2.2 billion basketball fans worldwide.

3

Sensational Superstars

Stephen Curry

Fans love the NBA's superstar players. Stephen Curry is one. He plays **point guard** for the Golden State Warriors. His fans love his energy. Curry is known for his shooting. He's made the most three-pointers in NBA history.

LeBron James is another fan favorite. He's been in the NBA since 2003. He has the most career points. He is known for his strength and power. James is one of basketball's **GOATs**.

Think About It Who is your favorite pro basketball player? What are their best skills?

LeBron James

4

Dramatic Dunks

Nate Robinson

One exciting basketball play is a slam dunk. Players jump high. Then they slam the ball into the hoop. The crowd goes wild! One of the NBA's best dunkers is Anthony Edwards. He soars through the air.

Every year, the NBA holds the Slam Dunk Contest. Players try challenging and creative dunks. Judges award points to their favorites. Nate Robinson has won three contests. He is only 5 foot 9 inches (1.75 meters) tall! That's short for most basketball players. He still does amazing dunks.

Think About It

Which takes more skill—a powerful dunk or a long three-pointer?

Nate Robinson

Welcome to the W

In 1996, the Women's National Basketball Association (WNBA) was started. The WNBA has many fans. There are currently 12 teams. The league has many star players. They have inspired many young women.

Sheryl Swoopes was a legend from the league's beginning. Maya Moore wowed fans in the 2010s. Today, young players like Caitlin Clark and Angel Reese amaze fans. More people than ever are watching basketball to follow the young WNBA players.

Maya Moore

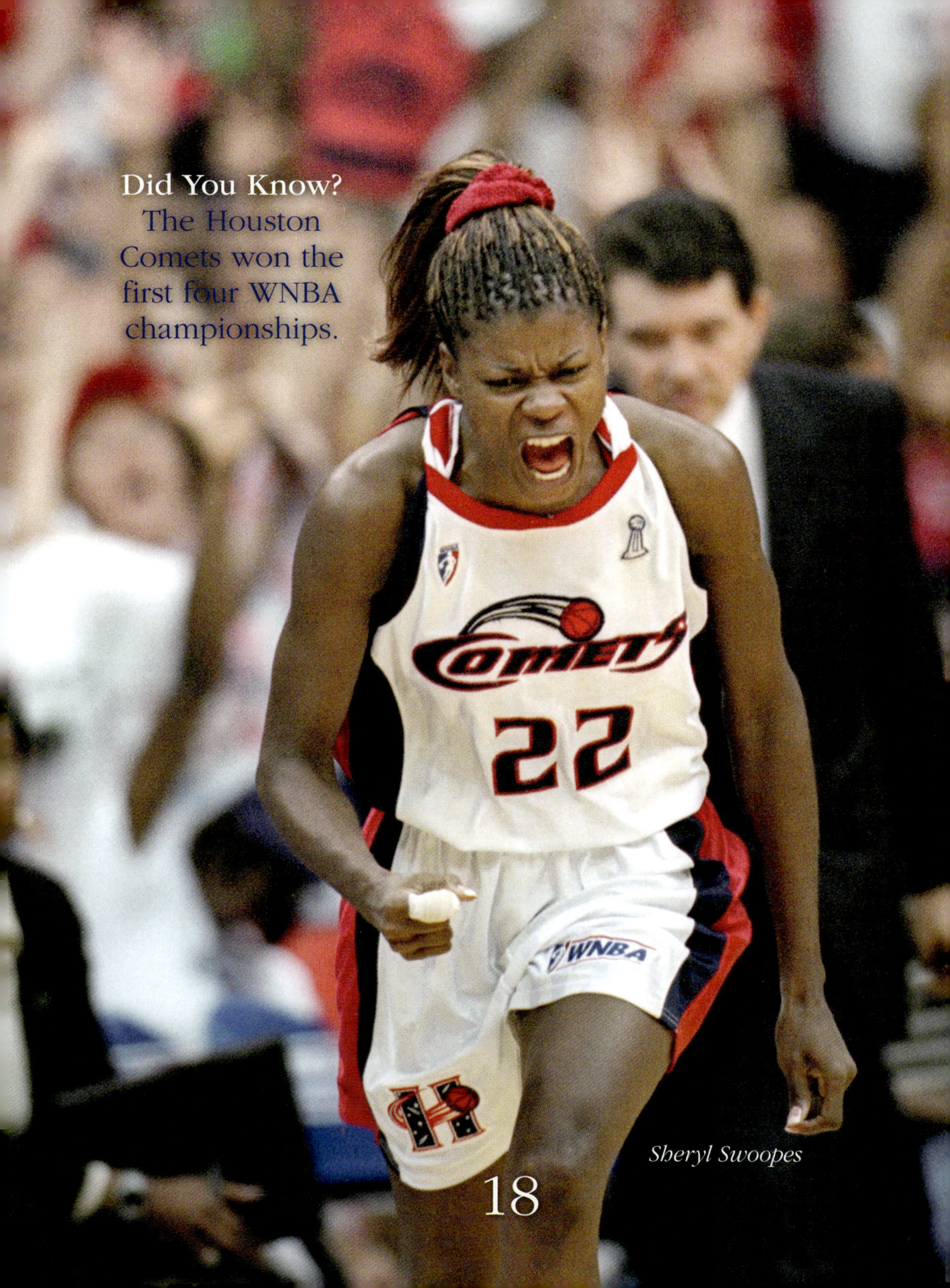

Did You Know?
The Houston Comets won the first four WNBA championships.

Sheryl Swoopes

6

March Madness

College basketball is also extremely popular. Each year, the season ends with March Madness. It is a tournament with all the best college teams. There is a men's and women's tournament. Millions of fans tune in to watch the "madness."

The best four teams play in the Final Four. The teams play inside football stadiums! Thousands of fans pack the stadium. They are proud of their schools. In the end, a national champion is crowned. Many college stars are drafted into the NBA or WNBA.

Did You Know?
UCLA has won the most men's basketball titles. UConn has the most women's titles.

MORE TO EXPLORE
FANTASTIC FACTS

The tallest WNBA player ever was Margo Dydek at 7 foot, 2 inches (2.2 meters).

An 89-foot (27-meter) shot by Baron Davis is the longest made basket in NBA history.

Diana Taurasi has played on Team USA six times. She helped her team win Olympic gold each time.

Kareem Abdul-Jabbar has the most NBA MVP awards with six.

In 1936, Joe Fortenberry was the first person to dunk in a game.

Wilt Chamberlain scored the most points ever in one game with 100!

MORE TO EXPLORE

COOL COMPARISONS

Which NBA and WNBA teams have the most championships?

(as of 2024)

MORE TO EXPLORE

RESOURCES

Glossary

draft (DRAFT) To pick a player for a professional team through a specialized system.

GOAT A person who is excellent or the best in their field; GOAT stands for "greatest of all time."

jumbotron (JUHM-boh-tron) A very large video display screen used in sports stadiums.

league (LEEG) A group of sports teams that play against each other.

point guard (POINT GAHRD) A player who is responsible for leading the team when trying to score.

Read More

Leed, Percy. *Basketball's NBA and WNBA Finals.* Minneapolis: Lerner Publications, 2025.

Thompson, Kim. *Caitlin Clark.* Mankato, MN: Amicus Learning, 2025.

Index

Clark, Caitlin, 16
college basketball, 20
Curry, Stephen, 10
Edwards, Anthony, 13
heights, 13, 22
history, 5, 22
James, LeBron, 10
Moore, Maya, 16
Reese, Angel, 16
Robinson, Nate, 13
slam dunks, 7, 13, 22
stadiums, 7, 20
Swoopes, Sheryl, 16
three-pointers, 7, 10
WNBA, 16, 18, 20, 22

TOP RANK is published by Black Rabbit Books, P.O. Box 227, Mankato, MN, 56002 • • Top Rank is an imprint of Black Rabbit Books. • Designed by Danny Nanos • Photographs © Associated Press/Darren Abate, 7, Darron Cummings, cover, 1; Getty Images/Christopher Hook/Icon Sportswire, 20, David Berding, 16, Greg Nelson 2, Jamie Squire, 19, Jed Jacobsohn, 14, Joe Buglewicz, 21, Kavin Mistry, 8–9, Leon Bennett, 17, Ronald Martinez, 11, 12–13, 18, Scott Wachter, 6; Shutterstock Andrey Burmakin, 4, New Africa, 23, Nigel Jarvis, 5, Oleksii Sidorov, cover, 1, Ruslan Ivantsov, 16, Victor Moussa, 13, zimmytws, 15 • Printed in India.
Library of Congress Cataloging-in-Publication Data: Names: Whitcomb, Aidan, author. | Title: Why we love basketball / by Aidan Whitcomb. | Description Mankato, MN : Black Rabbit Books, 2026. | Series: Why we love sports | Includes bibliographical references and index. | Ages 8–11 | Grades 2–3 | Identifiers: LCCN 2024050032 | ISBN 9781644668030 (library binding) | ISBN 9781644668351 (paperback) | ISBN 9781644668672 (ebook) | Subjects: LCSH: Basketball—Juvenile literature. | National Basketball Association—Juvenile literature. | Women's National Basketball Association—Juvenile literature. | Classification: LCC GV885. .W534 2026 | DDC 796.323—dc23/eng/20241118 | LC record available at https://lccn.loc.gov/2024050032